My Bodyworks

Songs about your bones, muscles, heart and more!

P9-CSW-460

By Jane Schoenberg

Music by Steven Schoenberg

Illustrations by Cynthia Fisher

CROCODILE BOOKS

An imprint of Interlink Publishing Group, Inc.

NEW YORK · NORTHAMPTON

For Sarah and Adam. And for Naomi and Mickey, too.
  —S&JS
For my sweet young friends, Will and Madeline
     —CF

First published in 2005 by

Crocodile Books
An imprint of Interlink Publishing Group, Inc.
46 Crosby Street, Northampton, Massachusetts 01060
www.interlinkbooks.com

Music and lyrics copyright © 2005, Jane and Steven Schoenberg
Illustrations copyright © 2005, Cynthia Fisher

All rights reserved. No part of this publication may be reproduced,
stored in a retrieval system, or transmitted in any form or by any
means, electronic, mechanical, photocopying, recording or otherwise
without the prior permission of the publisher.

Library of Congress Cataloging-in-Publication Data available
ISBN 1-56656-583-9
Designed by Barry Moser
Printed and bound in Canada

To request our complete 40-page full-color catalog, please call us toll
free at 1-800-238-LINK, visit our website at www.interlinkbooks.com
or send us an e-mail at info@interlinkbooks.com

My Bodyworks

BONES, BONES, BONES

(Chorus) Bones, bones, bones, bones, bones,
        Bones, bones, bones, bones, bones!

How many bones are in you and in me?
Why there're 206 bones, naturally.
Our bones hold us up and they keep us in line.
They make the backbone known as the spine.

    (Chorus)

Your bones are alive and they grow as you do.
They work with your muscles, allow you to move.
Bones are very strong but sometimes they do break.
Don't worry, they heal from the new bone they make.

    (Chorus)

There's fibula, tibia, humerus and radius,
Clavicle, scapula, vertebrae and skull.

    (Chorus)

There're 26 bones in each of your feet.
Your face has 14 bones — now isn't that neat?
Some are very tiny, some are very long;
So drink lots of milk and your bones will be strong.

    (Chorus)

There's fibula, tibia, humerus and radius,
Clavicle, scapula, vertebrae and skull.

    (Chorus)

IT'S YOUR MUSCLES

What makes you smile? What makes you frown?
What makes you stand and run or lie down?
What pulls your bones every time that you move?
What shapes you and makes up at least half of you?

(Chorus) It's your muscles, it's your muscles,
        It's your muscles, it's true.
        It's your muscles, it's your muscles,
        Your muscles help to move every part of you.

To blink an eye, swallow or sip,
To give a kiss, you pucker your lips.
To keep in shape you must exercise, too,
If you want your muscles to be strong for you.

(Chorus)

Bend down, reach out,
Flex, extend and walk about.
Stretching helps your muscles to improve.
Biceps, triceps, quadriceps and gluteus,
You can feel you're really in the groove!

Curl up your hands, wiggle your toes.
Blow a balloon, wrinkle your nose.
These are some things that your muscles can do.
Remember, your heart is a muscle, too!

(Chorus)

KEEP THE BEAT

Your heart never rests.
It continues to beat,
Sending blood to your head and your arms and your feet.
You can feel as it pumps
In your left upper chest,
Keeping you healthy so you do your best.

(Chorus) Your heart is at work when you play.
It never stops beating all through the day.
And even at night when you sleep,
Your heart's on the job keeping up with the beat —
With the beat!

Sometimes when you run,
You can feel your heart pound.
But, often, you don't even know it's around.
It's a muscle that's strong,
But you should exercise
To keep your heart healthy so you'll stay alive.

(Chorus)

Your heart never rests.
It continues to beat,
Sending blood to your head and your arms and your feet.
You can feel as it pumps
In your left upper chest,
Keeping you healthy so you do your best.

(Chorus)

TEETH ARE NEAT

In the morning when you wake up,
What's the first thing that you do?
You go into the bathroom,
Grab your toothbrush, and then you...

Just brush your teeth.
You brush your teeth.
Brush up and down and all around.
Just brush your teeth.

Now, you grow two sets of teeth.
This may seem funny, but it's true.
When you grow the second set,
Your teeth will number 32.

Teeth help you chew.
Teeth help you bite.
So brush your teeth morning and night,
Morning and night.

Please see a dentist twice a year,
Choose healthy foods to eat,
So every time you show your smile
Your teeth will look quite neat.

Did you know your teeth grow upward
From their roots down in your jaw?
The plaque that grows upon them
Causes cavities or flaws.

Keep your teeth clean
So when they're seen,
They'll look like new, last your life through.
Just brush your teeth!

Please see a dentist twice a year,
Choose healthy foods to eat,
So every time you show your smile
Your teeth will look quite neat.

In the morning when you wake up,
What's the first thing that you do?
You go into the bathroom,
Grab your toothbrush, and then you...

Just brush your teeth.
You brush your teeth.
Brush up and down and all around.
Just brush your teeth.

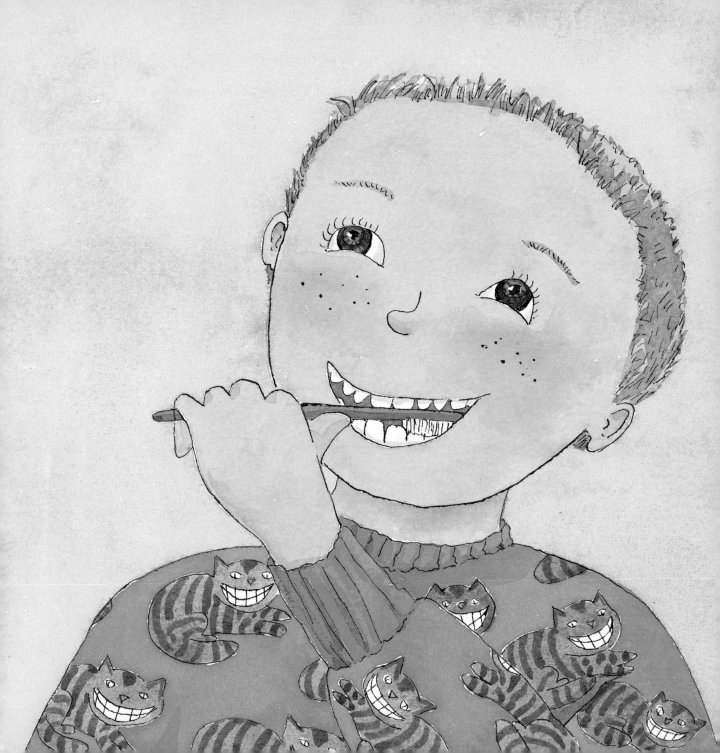

EVERYONE PASSES GAS

Last night at dinner I ate too much stuff.
I should have listened
When Mom said, "Enough."
Instead I kept eating and eating and eating
And eating and eating some more.
I ate 'til my tummy felt funny.
My tummy felt sore.

But soon I felt better.
I just didn't mind
When I heard some gas pass,
From somewhere behind.

I wasn't embarrassed.
I didn't feel shy.
'Cause everyone does it, yes, everyone does it.
The whole world does it
And I'll explain why.

When you swallow your food
It goes into your belly,
Where everything mixes to goopy-like jelly.
This is the start of digestion,
Which happens inside the intestines.

Good things like nutrients
Hang out all day,
While the things that you don't need
        get taken away.
The leftover stuff's now a gas,
Which comes out of you in a small blast.

When you swallow your food
It goes into your belly,
Where everything mixes to goopy-like jelly.
This is the start of digestion,
Which happens inside the intestines.

Good things like nutrients
Hang out all day,
While the things that you don't need
        get taken away.
The leftover stuff's now a gas,
Which comes out of you in a small blast.

So don't get embarrassed,
No need to feel shy.
Since everyone does it,
And now you know why.

Just say, "Excuse me,"
And leave it at that.
'Cause everyone, even Mom,
Everyone, definitely Dad,
Everyone passes, yes, everyone passes,
        the whole world passes…

WOOF! Even the dog…
Passes gas!

BRAINPOWER

(Chorus) You've got brainpower,
    You've got brainpower.
    Everybody's got it, everybody's got brainpower!

Your brain keeps sending messages right out,
Tells you to be quiet, and tells you when to shout,
Tells you when you're happy, tells you when you're sad,
Tells you when you're feeling hot or cold or hurting bad.

    (Chorus)

Directions from your brain tell your heart how fast to beat.
They travel through your body right down to your feet,
Direct you when to walk, direct you when to run,
Help you solve your problems, help you to have some fun.

    (Chorus)

It sends those special signals all through the day and night,
Tells you to breathe in and out and when to take a bite,
Allows you to create and imagine anything —
The brain within your head is, indeed, a wondrous thing!

    (Chorus)

Your lungs breathe in, your lungs breathe out.
They help you blow and they help you shout.
You always need to breathe to stay alive.
The air you breathe has oxygen;
Your body needs to take this in.
It's carbon dioxide that your lungs breathe out.

(Chorus) Inhale! Lungs expand just like a balloon,
          Changing, stretching like elastic.
          Exhale! All the air inside rushes out —
          It's awesome and fantastic!

It's healthier to breathe clean air.
The lungs are helped by little hairs,
Which work to keep all dust and smoke away.
Protect your lungs. Please, never smoke.
Remember, this is not a joke.
Keep your lungs clean and they'll work well for you.

    (Chorus)

Protect your lungs. Please, never smoke.
Remember, this is not a joke.
Keep your lungs clean and they'll work well for you.

    (Chorus)

AMAZING SENSES

How do you know what's hot or cold,
What's smooth or what feels rough,
What's squishy, gooey, hard or soft?
You know it by your touch.

(Chorus) It's just amazing to know
              That your senses are working for you.
              They let you see, hear and taste, touch and smell
              What is all around you.

How can you tell what's sour or sweet,
What's yummy or so-so,
What's salty, spicy, hot or bland?
Your taste will let you know!

              (Chorus)

You know what's cooking on the stove
Before you're in the room.
Your nose can tell by what it smells
That flowers are in bloom.

You've got two eyes that let you see the sky,
To know the color blue.
Your two ears let you hear this special song
That's written just for you.

              (Chorus)

HAVE FUN WITH YOUR HAIR

You can wash it or curl it,
Braid or unfurl it!
Color it blue, green or red.
You can cut it or grow it,
Hide it or show it.
It covers the top of your head.

You can buzz it, mohawk it,
Pigtail or dreadlock it!
Choose to be bald if you dare.
You can wig it or change it,
Ignore it, arrange it.
It's fun to have fun with your hair.

It's your hair —
Dress it up, dress it down,
Can be white, black or brown.
It's your hair!
It's your hair —
Long or short, old or new,
Makes you look different, too.
Your hair grows from follicles found in your skin.
Each day some falls out, each day some grows in.

You can brush it or comb it,
Cornrow it or foam it!
Gel it and style it with flair.
You can tease it or spray it,
Relax it or play it.
It's fun to have fun with your hair.

It's your hair —
Dress it up, dress it down,
Can be white, black or brown.
It's your hair!
It's your hair —
Long or short, old or new,
Makes you look different, too.
The hair on your head is fantastically strong,
If it never got cut it could be five feet long!

You can buzz it, mohawk it,
Pigtail or dreadlock it!
Choose to be bald if you dare.
You can wig it or change it,
Ignore it, arrange it.
It's fun to have fun with your hair.

Your body wears a cloak of skin.
It's what your skeleton's dressed in.
It covers everyone from head to toe.
It comes in different colors, too,
And grows each day along with you,
Protecting all your body parts within.

(*Chorus*) Your skin is so important.
       Be grateful to your skin.
       If you get cut, it heals itself
       By growing back again.

       Be careful of the sunshine,
       Try not to burn yourself.
       Your skin grows every day for you,
       It keeps you in good health.

Sometimes your skin feels itchy, ooh!
Or goosey bumpy, chilly, boo!
You dress it up with clothes or leave it bare.
Your face, your hands, your knees, your toes,
Your lips, your ears, even your nose —
Are covered by your skin, which grows your hair.

    (*Chorus*)

ON THE MOVE

Come on and bend down — turn around.
Now you can reach high — touch the sky.
Exercise your body today.

After you stretch out — jump about.
Then you can shake hips — really twist.
Exercise your body today.

(Chorus) So come on now, get in the groove.
       Keep your body on the move.
       One, two, three, four!
       This is great, let's do some more!

Climb up a tall slide, skip outside.
Go on a good hike, ride a bike.
Exercise your body today.

Play ball or run fast — what a blast!
Or try some hopscotch — don't just watch.
Exercise your body today.

    (Chorus)

Come on and bend down — turn around.
Now you can reach high — touch the sky.
Exercise your body today.

CELEBRATE OUR BODIES

Our bodies are a miracle,
In how they work and grow,
To start so small, and grow so tall,
And learn the things we know.

We all are very different,
And yet we're much the same.
Inside our skin are skeletons,
Inside our heads are brains.

(Chorus) Let's celebrate our bodies,
Be glad for who we are,
Because we're very special.
Indeed, we all are stars.

Our hearts pump blood throughout us.
Our lungs breathe night and day.
We touch and smell, our teeth chew well.
Our muscles help us play.

But still we all are different,
No fingerprint's the same.
We're all unique, the way we think.
We all have our own names.

(Chorus)

Each one of us is special,
The way we act and feel.
We all don't talk, we all don't walk,
But all have great appeal.

(Chorus)

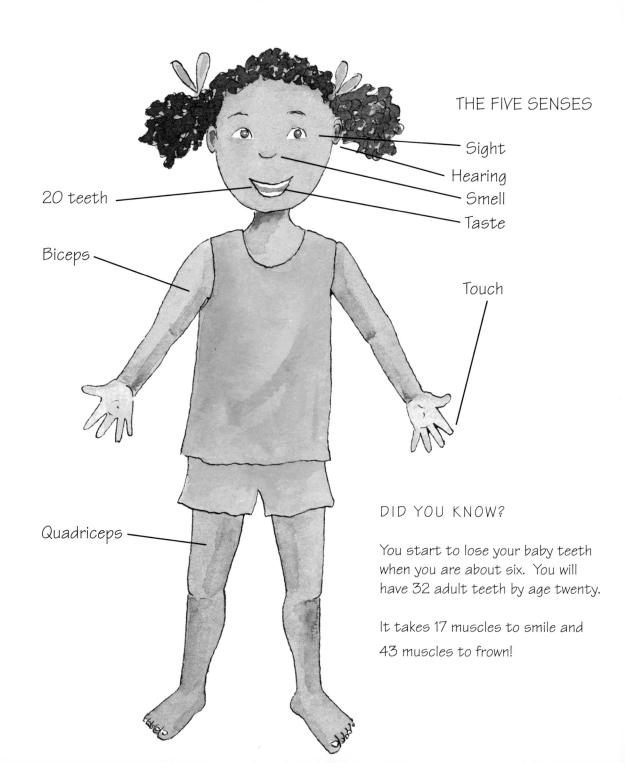

THE FIVE SENSES

Sight

Hearing

Smell

Taste

20 teeth

Biceps

Touch

Quadriceps

DID YOU KNOW?

You start to lose your baby teeth when you are about six. You will have 32 adult teeth by age twenty.

It takes 17 muscles to smile and 43 muscles to frown!

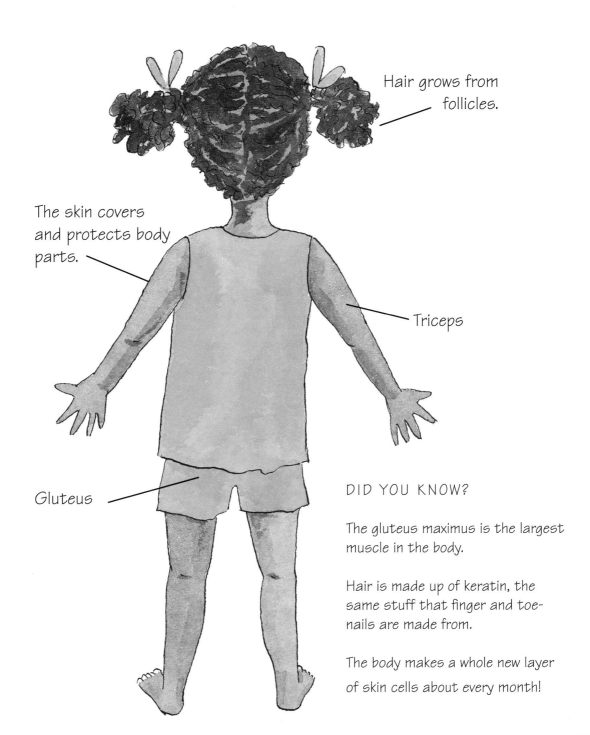

Hair grows from follicles.

The skin covers and protects body parts.

Triceps

Gluteus

DID YOU KNOW?

The gluteus maximus is the largest muscle in the body.

Hair is made up of keratin, the same stuff that finger and toe-nails are made from.

The body makes a whole new layer of skin cells about every month!

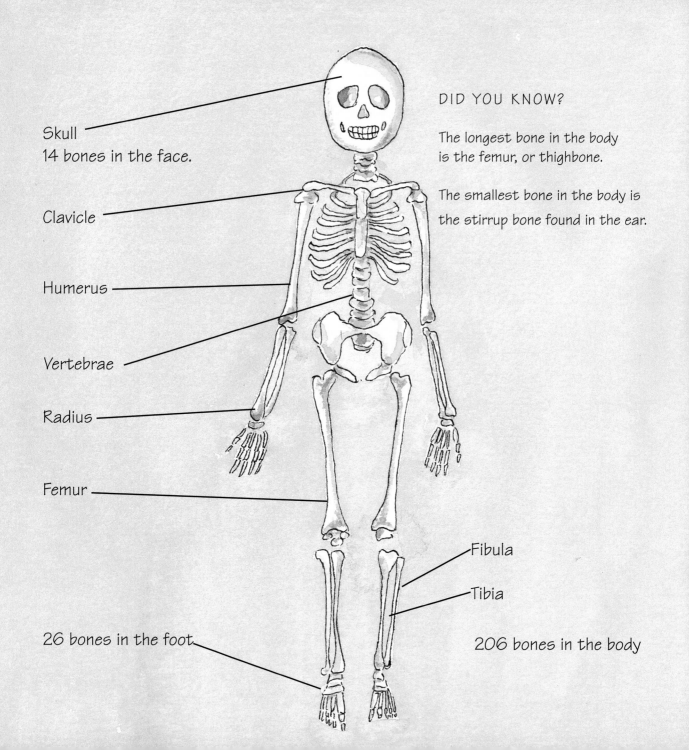

Skull
14 bones in the face.

Clavicle

Humerus

Vertebrae

Radius

Femur

26 bones in the foot.

DID YOU KNOW?

The longest bone in the body
is the femur, or thighbone.

The smallest bone in the body is
the stirrup bone found in the ear.

Fibula

Tibia

206 bones in the body

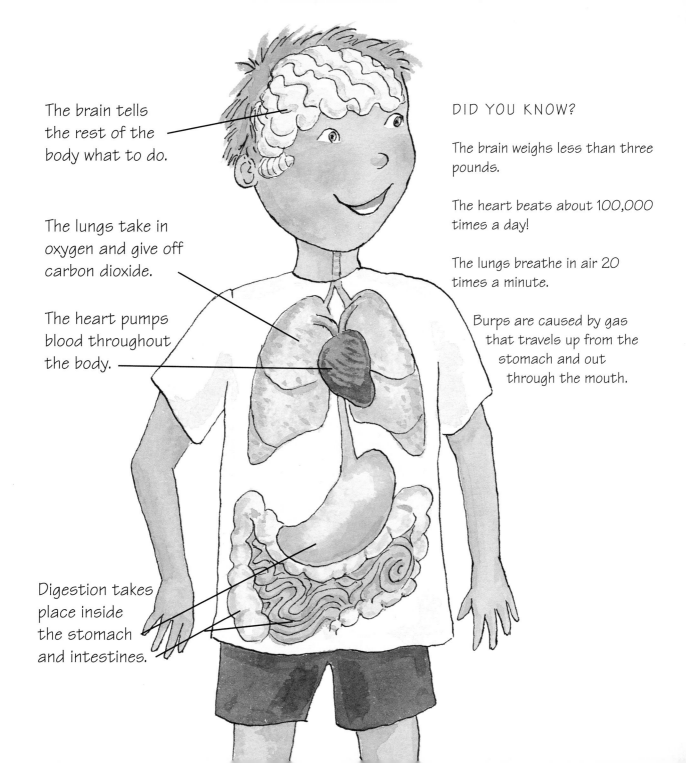

The brain tells the rest of the body what to do.

The lungs take in oxygen and give off carbon dioxide.

The heart pumps blood throughout the body.

Digestion takes place inside the stomach and intestines.

DID YOU KNOW?

The brain weighs less than three pounds.

The heart beats about 100,000 times a day!

The lungs breathe in air 20 times a minute.

Burps are caused by gas that travels up from the stomach and out through the mouth.

Compact Disc Credits:

Norman Blain, Lead Vocals & Harmonies; Leah Kunkel, Lead Vocals & Harmonies; Jane Schoenberg, Lead Vocal on "It's Your Muscles," & Harmonies; Steven Schoenberg, Lead Vocal on "Everyone Passes Gas" and "Have Fun With Your Hair," & Harmonies. Christopher Newland, All Acoustic & Electric Guitars; Guy DeVito, String Bass & All Electric Bass Guitars; Billy Klock, Drums; Steven Schoenberg, Piano & Synthesizer.

All songs written and produced by Steven and Jane Schoenberg

Engineered by Norman Blain; Mixed by Norman Blain and Steven Schoenberg

Mastered by Jim Hemingway, Shutesbury, MA

Special thanks to Naomi and Mickey Schoenberg, Adam Schoenberg, Barry Moser, Michel Moushabeck, David Sokol, Debbie Kramer, Wayne Cullinan, Carol Hillman, Michael Broad, René Nedelkoff and Thomas Hillman.

All songs © 2004 by EMME Music (ASCAP)

℗ © 2004 Quabbin Records, 10 Old Main Street, New Salem, MA 01355

Mokena Community
Public Library District